More Tunes You've Always Wanted To Play

arranged for piano by
Carol Barratt

CHESTER MUSIC
(A division of Music Sales Limited)
8/9 Frith Street, London W1V 5TZ.

Exclusive Distributors:
MUSIC SALES LIMITED
Distribution Centre:
Newmarket Road, Bury St. Edmunds,
Suffolk IP33 3YB.

		Page
AIR ON THE G STRING (Suite No. 3)	J. S. Bach	4
ALLELUIA (Exultate, Jubilate)	Mozart	6
BARBER OF SEVILLE, Themes from the Overture to The	Rossini	10
BARCAROLLE (The Tales of Hoffmann)	Offenbach	14
CANON	Pachelbel	16
CELLO CONCERTO, Theme from the	Elgar	20
CHORUS OF THE HEBREW SLAVES (Nabucco)	Verdi	22
CLARINET CONCERTO, Theme from the	Mozart	25
COPPÉLIA, Waltz from	Delibes	26
DANSE DES MIRLITONS (The Nutcracker)	Tchaikovsky	28
DEEP RIVER	American Spiritual	29
DIXIE LAND	Emmett	30
EINE KLEINE NACHTMUSIK, Themes from (Serenade in G major)	Mozart	31
ELEPHANT, The (The Carnival of the Animals)	Saint-Saëns	34
EVENING PRAYER (Hänsel and Gretel)	Humperdinck	36
FOUR SEASONS, Themes from The	Vivaldi	38
GAUDEAMUS IGITUR (The Academic Festival Overture)	Brahms	40
GOLLIWOG'S CAKE WALK (Children's Corner)	Debussy	41
GYMNOPÉDIE NO. 1	Satie	44
HORNPIPE (The Water Music)	Handel	46
HUMORESKE (Eight Humoreskes)	Dvořák	48
HUNGARIAN DANCE NO. 5	Brahms	50
LA DONNA È MOBILE (Rigoletto)	Verdi	52
LIBERTY BELL, The	Sousa	54
LIEBESTRAUM NO. 3 (Nocturne)	Liszt	57
LITTLE DAVID	American Spiritual	60
MARCH OF THE MEN OF HARLECH	Welsh Air	61
MARCHE MILITAIRE	Schubert	62
MARCHING THROUGH GEORGIA	Work	65
MELODY IN F	Rubinstein	66
MIKADO, Two tunes from The	Sullivan	69

		Page
MORNING *(Peer Gynt Suite)*	Grieg	72
MUSICAL JOKE, A	Mozart	74
OCTET, Theme from the	Schubert	76
PASTORAL SYMPHONY	Beethoven	77
PAVANE *(Capriol Suite)*	Warlock	80
PIE JESU *(Requiem)*	Fauré	84
POMP & CIRCUMSTANCE MARCH NO. 4, **Theme from**	Elgar	86
PRELUDE	Chopin	87
PROCESSION OF THE SARDAR *(Caucasian Sketches)*	Ippolitov-Ivanov	88
PROMENADE *(Pictures at an Exhibition)*	Mussorgsky	90
RULE, BRITANNIA	Arne	92
SAILORS' CHORUS *(The Flying Dutchman)*	Wagner	93
SARABANDE *(Suite XI)*	Handel	96
SEE, THE CONQUERING HERO COMES *(Judas Maccabaeus)*	Handel	99
SHEPHERDS' FAREWELL, The *(The Childhood of Christ)*	Berlioz	102
SICILIENNE	Fauré	104
SKYE BOAT SONG, The	Scottish Air	106
SONATA IN C, Theme from	Mozart	107
SWAN LAKE, Theme from	Tchaikovsky	110
SWING LOW, SWEET CHARIOT	American Spiritual	113
SYMPHONY NO. 1, Theme from	Brahms	114
SYMPHONY NO. 5 *(Theme from Death in Venice)*	Mahler	116
SYMPHONY NO. 40, Theme from	Mozart	118
TALES FROM THE VIENNA WOODS	J. Strauss II	122
TAMBOURIN	Gossec	126
TANGO	Albéniz	128
TOM BOWLING	Dibdin	131
TRISTESSE STUDY	Chopin	132
VARIATIONS ON A THEME OF HAYDN, **Theme from** *(St. Anthony Chorale)*	Brahms	134
WILLIAM TELL, Theme from the **Overture to**	Rossini	136
ZADOK THE PRIEST	Handel	139

AIR ON THE G STRING

from Suite No. 3

Johann Sebastian Bach
(1685–1750)

Andante espressivo

CH 58750

ALLELUIA

from the motet *Exultate, Jubilate (K.165)*

Wolfgang Amadeus Mozart
(1756–1791)

Allegro non troppo

CH 58750

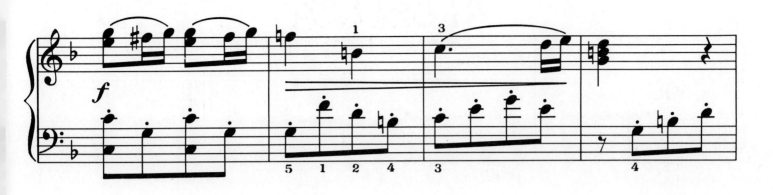

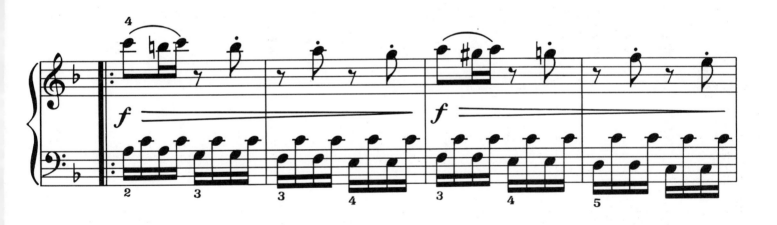

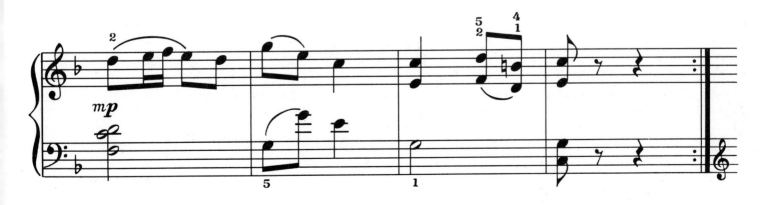

Themes from the Overture to
THE BARBER OF SEVILLE

Gioacchino Rossini
(1792–1868)

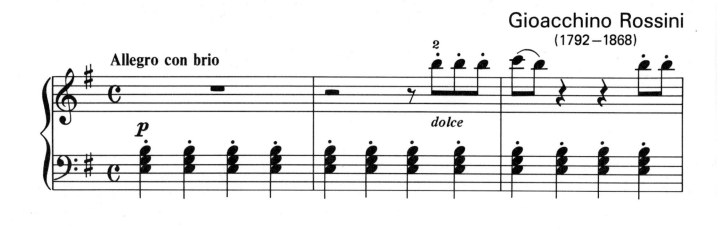

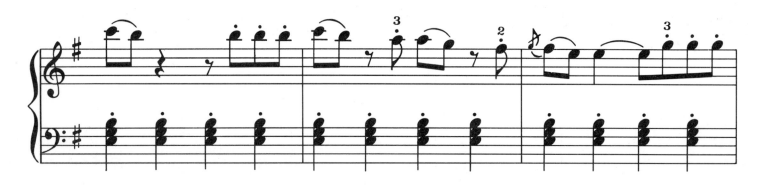

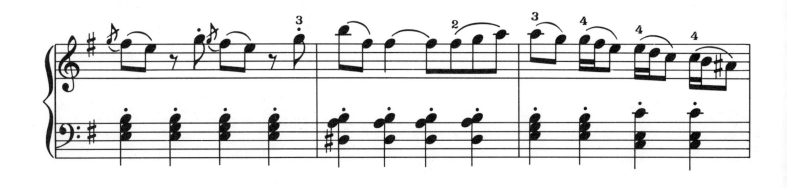

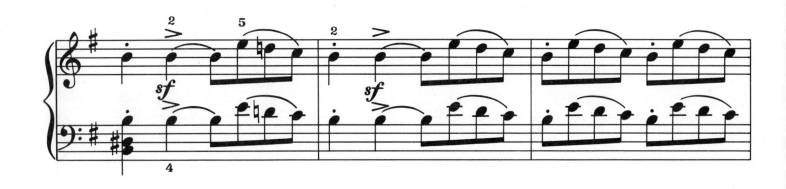

BARCAROLLE

from *The Tales of Hoffmann*

Moderato

Jacques Offenbach
(1819 – 1880)

pp leggiero

mp cantabile

con Ped.

1st time only

2nd time only

rit. *Fine*

pp

mp

CH 58750

D.S. al Fine

CANON

Johann Pachelbel
(1653–1706)

CH 58750

Con 8va ad lib..

Theme from the
CELLO CONCERTO

Edward Elgar
(1857–1934)

CH 58750

CHORUS OF THE HEBREW SLAVES

from *Nabucco*

Giuseppe Verdi
(1813–1901)

Theme from the
CLARINET CONCERTO

Wolfgang Amadeus Mozart
(1756–1791)

Waltz from
COPPÉLIA

Léo Delibes
(1836—1891)

Valse moderato

CH 58750

DANSE DES MIRLITONS

from *The Nutcracker*

Peter Ilich Tchaikovsky
(1840—1893)

CH 58750

DEEP RIVER

American Spiritual

CH 58750

DIXIE LAND

Daniel Decatur Emmett
(1815–1904)

CH 58750

Themes from
EINE KLEINE NACHTMUSIK

Serenade in G major (K. 525), first movement

Wolfgang Amadeus Mozart
(1756–1791)

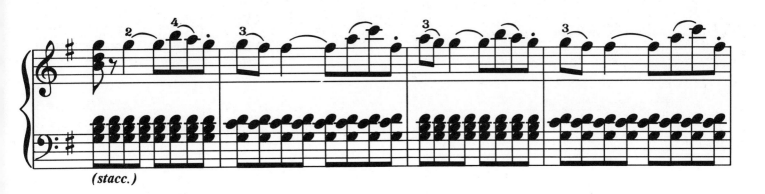

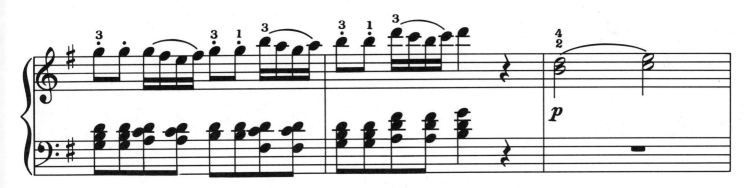

CH 58750

THE ELEPHANT

from *The Carnival of the Animals*

Camille Saint-Saëns
(1835–1921)

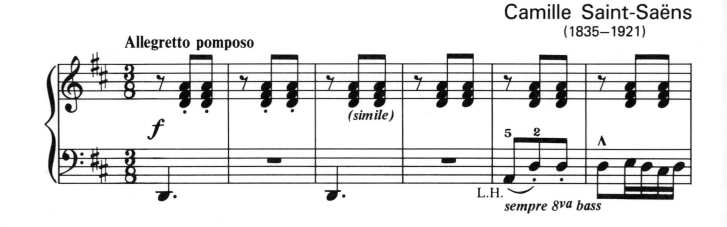

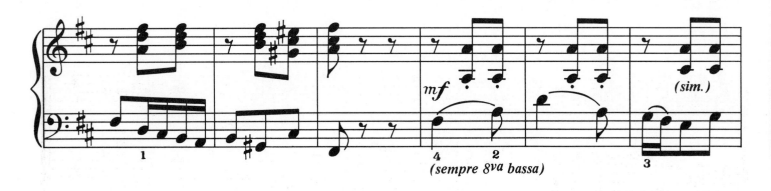

CH 58750

EVENING PRAYER

from *Hänsel and Gretel*

Engelbert Humperdinck
(1854–1921)

Themes from
THE FOUR SEASONS

1. Spring

Antonio Vivaldi
(1685–1741)

CH 58750

2. Autumn

GAUDEAMUS IGITUR

from *The Academic Festival Overture*

Johannes Brahms
(1833–1897)

CH 58750

GOLLIWOG'S CAKE WALK

from *Children's Corner*

Claude Debussy
(1862–1918)

Allegro giusto

CH 58750

8va bassa. . . . .

GYMNOPÉDIE NO. 1

Erik Satie
(1866–1925)

HORNPIPE

from *The Water Music*

George Frideric Handel
(1685–1759)

CH 58750

HUMORESKE

(No. 7 from *Eight Humoreskes*, Op. 101)

Antonin Dvořák
(1841–1904)

CH 58750

HUNGARIAN DANCE NO. 5

Johannes Brahms
(1833–1897)

LA DONNA È MOBILE

from *Rigoletto*

Giuseppe Verdi
(1813–1901)

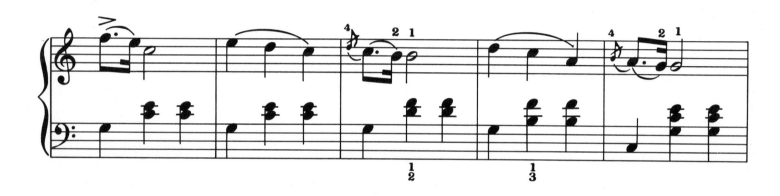

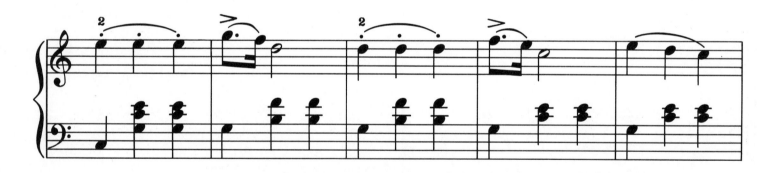

CH 58750

THE LIBERTY BELL

John Philip Sousa
(1854–1933)

CH 58750

LIEBESTRAUM NO. 3

Nocturne

Franz Liszt
(1811–1886)

CH 58750

58

LITTLE DAVID

American Spiritual

MARCH OF THE MEN OF HARLECH

Welsh Air

CH 58750

MARCHE MILITAIRE

Franz Schubert
(1797–1828)

Allegro vivace

CH 58750

MARCHING THROUGH GEORGIA

Henry Clay Work
(1832–1884)

CH 58750

MELODY IN F

Op. 3, No. 1

Anton Rubinstein
(1829–1894)

CH 58750

Two Tunes from
THE MIKADO
1. THE FLOWERS THAT BLOOM IN THE SPRING

Arthur Sullivan
(1842–1900)

CH 58750

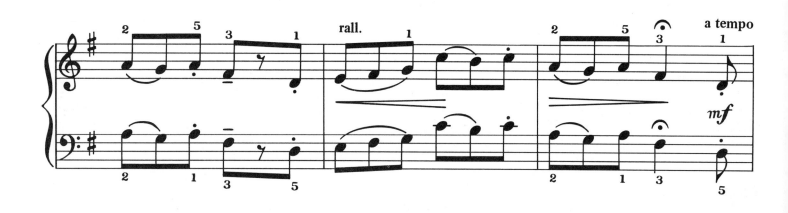

(Ped. _ _ _ _ _ _ _ _ _ _ ⌐)

2. WILLOW, TIT-WILLOW

MORNING

from *Peer Gynt Suite*

Edvard Hagerup Grieg
(1843–1907)

CH 58750

A MUSICAL JOKE

(K. 522, fourth movement)

Wolfgang Amadeus Mozart
(1756–1791)

Theme from the
OCTET

Franz Schubert
(1797–1828)

CH 58750

PASTORAL SYMPHONY

Theme from the 3rd Movement

Ludwig van Beethoven
(1770–1827)

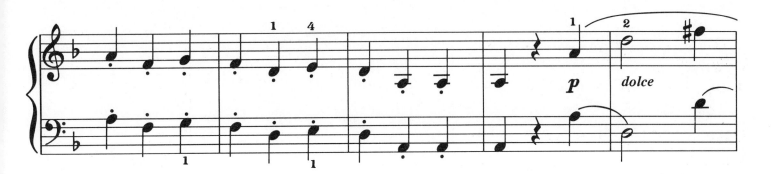

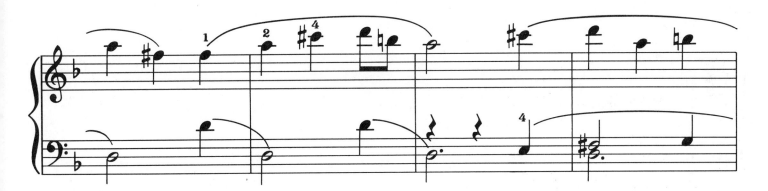

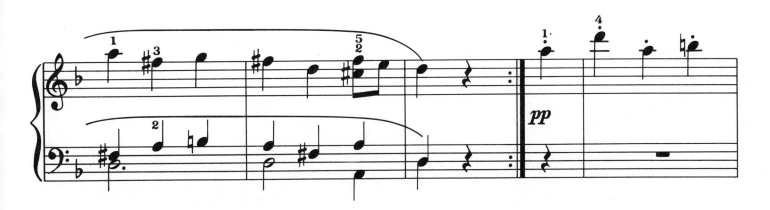

CH 58750

PAVANE

from the *Capriol Suite*

Peter Warlock
(1894–1930)

Allegretto, ma un poco lento

CH 58750

PIE JESU

from the Requiem

Gabriel Fauré
(1845–1924)

CH 58750

Theme from
POMP AND CIRCUMSTANCE
MARCH NO. 4

Edward Elgar
(1857–1934)

CH 58750

PRELUDE

Op. 28, No. 7.

Frédéric Chopin
(1810—1849)

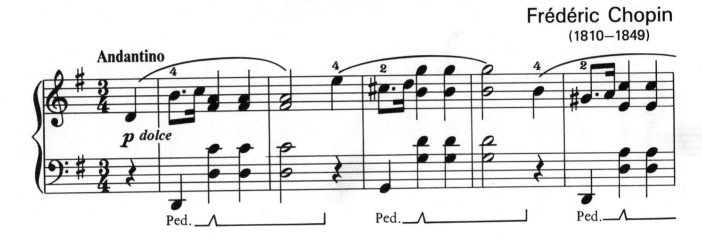

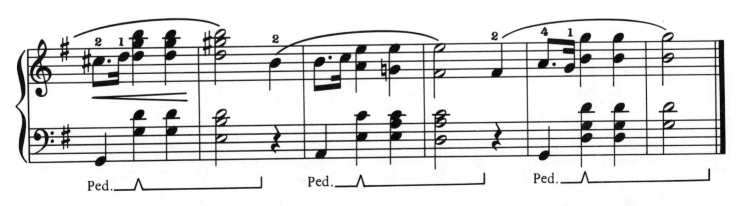

CH 58750

PROCESSION OF THE SARDAR

from *Caucasian Sketches*, Op. 10

Mikhail Ippolitov-Ivanov
(1859–1935)

Allegro moderato, tempo marziale

CH 58750

PROMENADE

from *Pictures at an Exhibition*

Modeste Mussorgsky
(1839–1881)

CH 58750

RULE, BRITANNIA

Thomas Augustine Arne
(1710–1778)

CH 58750

SAILORS' CHORUS

from *The Flying Dutchman*

Richard Wagner
(1813–1883)

CH 58750

SARABANDE

from Suite XI

George Frideric Handel
(1685–1759)

Andante con moto

CH 58750

Var. 1

Var. 2

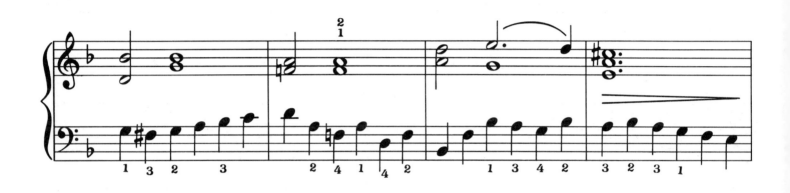

SEE, THE CONQUERING HERO COMES

from *Judas Maccabaeus*

George Frideric Handel
(1685–1759)

Allegro moderato

CH 58750

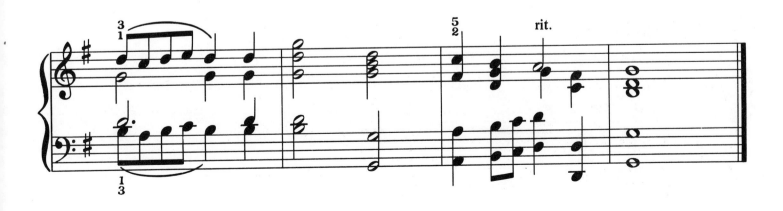

THE SHEPHERDS' FAREWELL

from *The Childhood of Christ*

Hector Berlioz
(1803–1869)

CH 58750

SICILIENNE

Gabriel Fauré
(1845–1924)

CH 58750

THE SKYE BOAT SONG

Scottish Air

CH 58750

Theme from
SONATA IN C

(K. 545, first movement)

Wolfgang Amadeus Mozart
(1756–1791)

CH 58750

Theme from
SWAN LAKE

Peter Ilich Tchaikovsky
(1840–1893)

CH 58750

SWING LOW, SWEET CHARIOT

American Spiritual

CH 58750

Theme from
SYMPHONY NO. 1

Finale

Johannes Brahms
(1833–1897)

Allegro non troppo

CH 58750

SYMPHONY NO. 5

3rd Movement
(Theme from *Death in Venice*)

Gustav Mahler
(1860–1911)

CH 58750

SYMPHONY No. 40

Theme from 1st movement

Wolfgang Amadeus Mozart
(1756–1791)

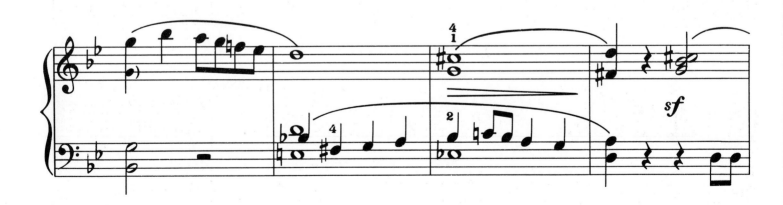

TALES FROM THE VIENNA WOODS

Johann Strauss II
(1825–1899)

CH 58750

TAMBOURIN

François Joseph Gossec
(1734–1829)

CH 58750

TANGO

Isaac Albéniz
(1860–1909)

CH 58750

TOM BOWLING

Charles Dibdin
(1745–1814)

CH 58750

TRISTESSE STUDY

Op. 10, No. 3

Frédéric Chopin
(1810–1849)

Lento ma non troppo

legato

Con ped.

cresc.

stretto

rit.

a tempo

Theme from
VARIATIONS ON A
THEME OF HAYDN

(St. Anthony Chorale)

Johannes Brahms
(1833–1897)

Theme from the Overture to
WILLIAM TELL

Gioacchino Rossini
(1792–1868)

CH 58750

ZADOK THE PRIEST

George Frideric Handel
(1685—1759)

Also available:

Tunes You've Always Wanted To Play

AIDA, Grand March from	Verdi
ALL THROUGH THE NIGHT	Welsh Air
ARIOSO	J. S. Bach
ASH GROVE, The	Welsh Air
AULD LANG SYNE	Scottish Air
AVE MARIA	Gounod
AVE MARIA	Schubert
BERCEUSE	Fauré
BLUE DANUBE, The	J. Strauss II
BLUEBELLS OF SCOTLAND, The	Scottish Air
BOURRÉE & AIR (Water Music)	Handel
BRIDAL MARCH (Lohengrin)	Wagner
BRITISH GRENADIERS, The	English Air
LA CALINDA, Themes from (Koanga)	Delius
CAN-CAN (Orpheus in the Underworld)	Offenbach
CARMEN, Themes from	Bizet
CHANSON DE MATIN	Elgar
CHARLIE IS MY DARLING	Scottish Air
CLAIR DE LUNE	Debussy
COCKLES AND MUSSELS	Irish Air
CUCKOO, The	Daquin
DANCE OF THE HOURS (La Gioconda)	Ponchielli
DAVID OF THE WHITE ROCK	Welsh Air
DRINK TO ME ONLY	English Air
ELVIRA MADIGAN, Theme from (Piano Concerto No. 21)	Mozart
ENGLISH COUNTRY GARDEN	English Air
FIFTH SYMPHONY, Theme from the	Beethoven
FOR HE IS AN ENGLISHMAN (H.M.S. Pinafore)	Sullivan
FÜR ELISE	Beethoven
GREENSLEEVES	English Air
HARMONIOUS BLACKSMITH, The	Handel
I VOW TO THEE, MY COUNTRY from Jupiter (The Planets)	Holst
JERUSALEM	Parry
LAND OF HOPE AND GLORY (Pomp and Circumstance)	Elgar
LARGO (Xerxes)	Handel

LONDONDERRY AIR, The	Irish Air
MÉDITATION (Thaïs)	Massenet
MINSTREL BOY, The	Irish Air
MINUET	Boccherini
MOONLIGHT SONATA, Theme from the	Beethoven
NEW WORLD SYMPHONY, **Themes from the**	Dvořák
NIMROD ("Enigma" Variations)	Elgar
NOCTURNE	Borodin
O, FOR THE WINGS OF A DOVE	Mendelssohn
O, MY BELOVED FATHER (Gianni Schicchi)	Puccini
ODE TO JOY (Choral Symphony)	Beethoven
ON WINGS OF SONG	Mendelssohn
PATHÉTIQUE SONATA, **Theme from the**	Beethoven
PAVANE	Fauré
PIANO CONCERTO NO. I, Theme from	Tchaikovsky
PILGRIMS' CHORUS (Tannhäuser)	Wagner
PIRATES OF PENZANCE, **Two Tunes from The**	Sullivan
POLOVTSIAN DANCES, Theme from (Prince Igor)	Borodin
RADETZKY MARCH	J. Strauss I
ROMEO AND JULIET, Theme from	Tchaikovsky
ROSAMUNDE, Entr'acte and Ballet Music	Schubert
SERENADE	Schubert
SHEEP MAY SAFELY GRAZE (Cantata No. 208)	J. S. Bach
SOLFEGGIETTO	C. P. E. Bach
SWAN, The	Saint-Saëns
SWAN LAKE, Waltz from	Tchaikovsky
TO A WILD ROSE	MacDowell
TRUMPET VOLUNTARY	Clarke
TWO SONGS: Rose among the Heather and To Music	Schubert
UNFINISHED SYMPHONY, Theme from	Schubert
VLTAVA, Theme from (Má Vlast)	Smetana
WEDDING MARCH (A Midsummer Night's Dream)	Mendelssohn
WHERE'ER YOU WALK	Handel

Printed and bound in Great Britain by
Dotesios Ltd, Trowbridge, Wiltshire.